WEATHER REPORT

WEATHER REPORT

A 90-day journal for reflection
and well-being, with the aid of
the Beaufort Wind Scale

MARGARET
O'BRIEN

ISBN: 978-1-3999-3451-0

Concept and text by Margaret O'Brien (margaretaobrien.com).

Beaufort Wind Scale illustrations by Monty Pyle (Twitter: @mordhiobhail).

Book design by Gwarlingo Studio (gwarlingostudio.com).

Back cover author photo by Monika Grabowska Photography (monikagrabowska.com).

Mark Roper, quote from the poem, "Just" in *A Gather of Shadow*, Dedalus Press, 2012, courtesy of the author.

Mark Roper, quote from the poem, "A Far Cry" in *Bindweed*, Dedalus Press, 2017, courtesy of the author.

Writing Changes Lives
Margaret A. O'Brien

Scale of Winds,
Or key to the wind column in this Log.

1   Light air   Or, that which just enables a ship to steer.
2   Light breeze   Or, that which will impel a man of war with all sail   3 to 4 knots
3   Gentle breeze   Or,   Do   Do   4 to 5
4   Moderate breeze   Or,   Do   Do   5 to 6
5   Fresh breeze   Or, that with which whole Tt. royals, stay.t &c. may be just carried full & by
6   Stiff breeze   Or, that with which single reefed Tt. & Tg.t courses, jib, & driver would be just carried by the wind, by a close reefed frigate, when fairly rigged in chase
7   Moderate gale   Or, that with which the same vessel would just set 2d. reefs Tt. and jib
8   Fresh gale   Or, that where the same ship could barely carry 3d. reefs Tt. & courses
9   Strong gale   Or, that when she would beat off a lee shore with reefed courses & close reefed fore and main topsails.
10 A whole gale   Or, that when she could spread no other canvas than storm stay sails.
11 Storm   Or, that which would blow away any sails made in the usual way
12 Hurricane   Hurricane!

Key to the abbreviations in the weather column,
in the following log.

b. Blue Sky.	gl. Gloomy overloaded Sky.	p. Passing Clouds
c. Clear horizon, distant objects distinct.	gr. Greasy.	r. Rain
cl. Cloudy.	h. Hazy	sh. Showery
da. Damp atmosphere.	hsh. Hard showers	sq. Squalls
dk. Dark heavy weather.	hr. Heavy rain	sr. Small rain
dr. Drizzling	hsq. Hard squalls	t. Thunder
f. Fair	l. Lightning	thr. Threatening appearance
fg Thick fog	m. Misty.	w. Watery Sky
fgy Foggy		wh. White dazzling haze

 *INTRODUCTION*

Welcome to *Weather Report*, a reflective journal that uses the Beaufort Wind Scale as a tool for health and well-being.

The Beaufort Wind Scale is a simple scale that charts the force of the wind from 1 to 12, with clear and specific visual indicators for each point on the scale.

For example: 1 on the scale is a state of complete calm, which is illustrated by 'smoke rising vertically from chimneys'; while at 5 there is more movement of air and 'branches of trees moving, hair blowing'. The wind intensifies all the way to 12, which is a period of high winds and results in 'devastation and widespread damage'.

Weather Report has been designed so that the scale will also give you an entry point to your own inner weather, which can be similarly changeable. The prompts here for each day are an open invitation to you to identify how you are, using the points on the Beaufort Wind Scale as a reference, then also briefly noting what you feel, what you think and what you did. You will also find here a daily invitation to notice beauty in your day and the opportunity for a guided weekly reflection.

The illustrations on the following pages, drawn especially for this journal by artist Monty Pyle, show each point on the scale in a direct and simple way that you can use as a reference as you complete each day's entry.

As I write this, there is beautiful weather for March here in Ireland. To frame it using the Beaufort Scale, today's weather is to me a 1 - perfectly calm, with not even a whisper of a breeze to disturb a leaf and any smoke that is visible rises straight up from the chimneys. What else can I see? There is a blackbird hopping around outside, looking for worms, the daffodils in a Guinness pint glass are brightening my kitchen window. Now what do I hear? From somewhere nearby there is the sound of a lawn-mower engine, also birdsong and now a message pops into my phone with a ping. However, that is all external to me. Now what about my internal weather, what am I noticing in me? Hmmm - to be honest I feel a little bit of agitation, a worry about expressing myself here in writing so that my meaning is clear to anyone, to everyone. My mouth feels a bit dry, I hadn't realised it. I go to the fridge and fill a glass of water to sip on while I work. I decide to work on this for about another twenty minutes, and then come back to it later with a fresh mind. My guess is that on the Beaufort Scale my internal weather would have been a 4 at the start, feeling a bit fraught, but now all this noticing in the past couple of minutes has calmed me down a little. Now I'm closer to a 2 or maybe a 3, with a certain amount of nervous energy that feels good, which might now be channelled in a productive way.

As you can see the external weather, what is happening outside, and the internal weather, my emotional state, can be quite different. But the simple act of noticing, of becoming aware of the latter makes subtle and beneficial change possible.

Being prompted to bring your attention to small moments in your day can be a simple route to profound change over time. That is the process you will engage in as you complete each day's page.

BEAUTY

In her book, *Bittersweet*, Susan Cain writes of the necessity to 'turn in the direction of beauty' and to know that 'beauty [is] a state we can access'. This 'turn' in our attention to what is beautiful in the world, is the aim of the daily Message to Myself, which gives you space to write or draw one thing you identified as beautiful in your day.

Writer Elaine Scarry reminds us that, "Beauty always takes place in the particular." When artist Sheila Wood was using the prototype of *Weather Report*, she found herself struggling one day to recall a moment of beauty to complete her day's entry (this from a consummate artist who produces profoundly beautiful and moving work). Then she remembered! She had that morning seen a blue butterfly on a patch of grass, which she and her husband Ken had allowed to grow wild. In our conversation it was obvious to me that Sheila had experienced real delight in noticing the blue butterfly earlier in her day but the delight was repeated later as she expressed it in writing into her copy of *Weather Report*, and further intensified as she recounted it to me. Her face and physical demeanour became animated with the restored pleasure of that blue butterfly and the opportunity to share it now with me.

In Mary Oliver's poem, "Don't Hesitate," she closes with the line, "Joy is not meant to be a crumb." Our small 'noticings' of joy, of beauty, inevitably have a tendency to gather positive energy; think of Sheila Wood's blue butterfly. Over time, these crumbs of joy have the potential to become amplified and spill their beauty into other aspects of daily living.

In addition to the daily pages, you will find at the end of each week the opportunity to do a 'Weekly Reflection'. This is a page for you to pause and identify three small things that went well for you in the past week. Then you follow that by identifying why each went well. This latter part is very important. It is a way of identifying the actions you took that set good things in motion in your life. It is a very crucial element of this practice. To close the Weekly Reflection you will see an invitation to identify something you are looking forward to doing in the next week. Again this has benefits in terms of building optimism and strengthening your sense of agency in the world.

Sir Francis Beaufort, who developed the initial wind scale as an aid to mariners, was an Irishman who lived from 1774 to 1857 and who became rear-admiral of the British Royal Navy. Among many things in his remarkable life, he was the person who was instrumental in gaining permission for Charles Darwin to travel on board The Beagle on its voyage to circumnavigate South America and then the globe. It was out of this experience that Darwin's most momentous scientific work flowed. You will see included, on the page opposite Day 72, a quote from Darwin, "The mind is a chaos of delight", which he wrote into his journal as he made the homeward journey on board The Beagle, his mind filled with the wonders of his observations and experiences on this remarkable round-the-world voyage.

Beaufort once said: 'the tendency of all people is to undervalue what they do not understand'. As you complete each day's entry in *Weather Report* it may not be entirely clear to you how the process is working, but despite that I invite you to heed Francis Beaufort's words and not undervalue the work you do between the pages of this journal. Beaufort's legacy, the wind scale, is after all the result of his attention to detail, noticing and then recording his observations in his journals.

Similarly, if you do the simple daily exercises in *Weather Report* over the coming ninety days, you will discover through noticing and naming, by even momentarily paying attention, that this practice will work its magic for you in subtly beneficial and at times surprising ways.

HOW TO USE THIS JOURNAL

I invite you to write, to draw, to doodle; perhaps use colour on the pages. In my experience, short periods (even a couple of minutes) of this kind of attention can be of more benefit than you might expect. Don't feel that you have to give big blocks of time to it. Remember, this journal is for YOU to use in any way you find helpful. But do use it and make your own discoveries about the transformative power of noticing, of reflecting and of the creative arts.

- Make time: you have the gift of this journal in your hands; now make a little time each day to enter your observations and experiences in response to the prompts.

- Prepare: each day settle yourself somewhere comfortable, take a breath, find a moment of stillness in yourself to complete your 'Weather Report'.

- Persist: aim to do it every day, but if you miss a day or two simply start over. Be kind to yourself.

- Connect: and re-connect with the moments in the world outside, and your own inner world.

- Observe: how this simple act of noticing and recording impacts on you over time.

- Remember: as Mary Oliver wrote; "Joy is not meant to be a crumb."

Weather Report has been designed to be simple to use and to give you an indirect, but powerful route towards living with strength, energy and joy.

Welcome,

Margaret

THE BEAUFORT WIND SCALE

Illustrations by Monty Pyle

Smoke rises vertically.

Smoke drifts.

Leaves rustle. Breeze felt on face.

Leaves and twigs move.

Branches move. Hair blows.

Small trees sway. Smoke is
almost horizontal.

OUTER WEATHER

Large branches move.
Umbrellas used with difficulty.

Whole trees move. Hold onto
your hat.

Twigs break. Walking is difficult.

Signs, chimney pots, etc. get
blown down.

Trees uprooted. Considerable
damage to buildings.

Countryside is devastated.
Widespread damage.

THERE IS NO DAY

WITHOUT

its moments of

PARADISE.

—Jorge Luis Borges

OUTER WEATHER

Beaufort Scale # _____ Time of day _____

What can you see? What can you hear?
What can you feel?
Write or draw your observations...

Day 2

Day _____

Date _____

INNER WEATHER

Beaufort Scale # _____ Time of day _____

What I feel? Where in my body do I feel it?
What I think? What I did?
Write or draw what you notice...

MESSAGE
TO MYSELF

*Write or draw here one
thing I found beautiful today...*

MOMENTS OF

BEAUTY

begin to braid

YOUR DAYS.

—John O'Donohue

OUTER WEATHER

Day 3

Beaufort Scale # _____ Time of day _____

What can you see? What can you hear?
What can you feel?
Write or draw your observations...

Day _____

Date _____

INNER WEATHER

Beaufort Scale # _____ Time of day _____

What I feel? Where in my body do I feel it?
What I think? What I did?
Write or draw what you notice...

MESSAGE
TO MYSELF

*Write or draw here one
thing I found beautiful today...*

A TINCTURE OF
POSSIBILTY...

—Sebastian Barry

OUTER WEATHER

Beaufort Scale # _____ Time of day _____

What can you see? What can you hear?
What can you feel?
Write or draw your observations...

Day 4

Day _____

Date _____

INNER WEATHER

Beaufort Scale # _____ Time of day _____

What I feel? Where in my body do I feel it?
What I think? What I did?
Write or draw what you notice...

MESSAGE
TO MYSELF

*Write or draw here one
thing I found beautiful today...*

OUTER WEATHER

Beaufort Scale # _____ Time of day _____

What can you see? What can you hear?
What can you feel?
Write or draw your observations...

Day 5

Day _____

Date _____

INNER WEATHER

Beaufort Scale # _____ Time of day _____

What I feel? Where in my body do I feel it?
What I think? What I did?
Write or draw what you notice...

MESSAGE
TO MYSELF

*Write or draw here one
thing I found beautiful today...*

IN THIS BOOK

THERE

are many

HUMMINGBIRDS

—Mary Oliver

OUTER WEATHER

Day 6

Beaufort Scale # _____ Time of day _____

What can you see? What can you hear?
What can you feel?
Write or draw your observations...

Day _____

Date _____

INNER WEATHER

Beaufort Scale # _____ Time of day _____

What I feel? Where in my body do I feel it?
What I think? What I did?
Write or draw what you notice...

MESSAGE
TO MYSELF

*Write or draw here one
thing I found beautiful today...*

SOME THINGS ARE

UP TO US

and some are

NOT UP TO US.

—Epictetus

OUTER WEATHER

Day 7

Beaufort Scale # _____ Time of day _____

What can you see? What can you hear?
What can you feel?
Write or draw your observations...

Day _____

Date _____

INNER WEATHER

Beaufort Scale # _____ Time of day _____

What I feel? Where in my body do I feel it?
What I think? What I did?
Write or draw what you notice...

MESSAGE TO MYSELF

*Write or draw here one
thing I found beautiful today...*

Weekly Reflection 1

Write down three small things that went well for you this week.

1.

2.

3.

Write down WHY each went well (this is a crucial step). For example, "I asked for help"; "I arranged to meet a friend for a walk"; "I allowed myself to cry and then had a drink of water," etc.

1.

2.

3.

Write down something you're looking forward to doing in the next week.

WHAT WE

DREAM

of is already

PRESENT IN THE

WORLD.

—Rebecca Solnit

OUTER WEATHER

Beaufort Scale # _____ Time of day _____

What can you see? What can you hear?
What can you feel?
Write or draw your observations...

Day 8

Day _____

Date _____

INNER WEATHER

Beaufort Scale # _____ Time of day _____

What I feel? Where in my body do I feel it?
What I think? What I did?
Write or draw what you notice...

MESSAGE
TO MYSELF

*Write or draw here one
thing I found beautiful today...*

WALK ON AIR

AGAINST

your better

JUDGMENT.

—Seaumus Heaney

OUTER WEATHER

Day 9

Beaufort Scale # _____ Time of day _____

What can you see? What can you hear?
What can you feel?
Write or draw your observations...

Day _____

Date _____

INNER WEATHER

Beaufort Scale # _____ Time of day _____

What I feel? Where in my body do I feel it?
What I think? What I did?
Write or draw what you notice...

MESSAGE
TO MYSELF

*Write or draw here one
thing I found beautiful today...*

OUTER WEATHER

Day 10

Beaufort Scale # _____ Time of day _____

What can you see? What can you hear?
What can you feel?
Write or draw your observations...

Day _____

Date _____

INNER WEATHER

Beaufort Scale # _____ Time of day _____

What I feel? Where in my body do I feel it?
What I think? What I did?
Write or draw what you notice...

MESSAGE
TO MYSELF

*Write or draw here one
thing I found beautiful today...*

...MOVE FORWARD WITH

God's reckless

WOBBLE.

—Galway Kinnell,
from the poem "Oatmeal"

OUTER WEATHER

Beaufort Scale # _____ Time of day _____

What can you see? What can you hear?
What can you feel?
Write or draw your observations...

Day 11

Day _____

Date _____

INNER WEATHER

Beaufort Scale # _____ Time of day _____

What I feel? Where in my body do I feel it?
What I think? What I did?
Write or draw what you notice...

MESSAGE
TO MYSELF

*Write or draw here one
thing I found beautiful today...*

THE WORLD IS

DOUBLED

by play.

—John Berger

OUTER WEATHER

Beaufort Scale # _____ Time of day _____

What can you see? What can you hear?
What can you feel?
Write or draw your observations...

Day 12

Day _____

Date _____

INNER WEATHER

Beaufort Scale # _____ Time of day _____

What I feel? Where in my body do I feel it?
What I think? What I did?
Write or draw what you notice...

MESSAGE TO MYSELF

*Write or draw here one
thing I found beautiful today...*

POETRY

arrived

TO LOOK FOR ME.

—Pablo Neruda

OUTER WEATHER

Day 13

Beaufort Scale # _____ Time of day _____

What can you see? What can you hear?
What can you feel?
Write or draw your observations...

Day _____

Date _____

INNER WEATHER

Beaufort Scale # _____ Time of day _____

What I feel? Where in my body do I feel it?
What I think? What I did?
Write or draw what you notice...

MESSAGE
TO MYSELF

*Write or draw here one
thing I found beautiful today...*

PRESENT

MOMENT,

wonderful

MOMENT.

—Thich Nhat Hanh

OUTER WEATHER

Beaufort Scale # _____ Time of day _____

What can you see? What can you hear?
What can you feel?
Write or draw your observations...

Day 14

Day _____

Date _____

INNER WEATHER

Beaufort Scale # _____ Time of day _____

What I feel? Where in my body do I feel it?
What I think? What I did?
Write or draw what you notice...

MESSAGE
TO MYSELF

*Write or draw here one
thing I found beautiful today...*

Weekly Reflection 2

Write down three small things that went well for you this week.

1.

2.

3.

Write down WHY each went well (this is a crucial step). For example, "I asked for help"; "I arranged to meet a friend for a walk"; "I allowed myself to cry and then had a drink of water," etc.

1.

2.

3.

Write down something you're looking forward to doing in the next week.

IT IS THE

STORY

that makes the

DIFFERENCE.

—Ursula K. Le Guin

OUTER WEATHER

Beaufort Scale # _____ Time of day _____

What can you see? What can you hear?
What can you feel?
Write or draw your observations...

Day 15

Day _____

Date _____

INNER WEATHER

Beaufort Scale # _____ Time of day _____

What I feel? Where in my body do I feel it?
What I think? What I did?
Write or draw what you notice...

MESSAGE TO MYSELF

*Write or draw here one
thing I found beautiful today...*

GIVE US THE

the whole

MOSAIC.

—John Hewitt

OUTER WEATHER

Day 16

Beaufort Scale # _____ Time of day _____

What can you see? What can you hear?
What can you feel?
Write or draw your observations...

Day _____

Date _____

INNER WEATHER

Beaufort Scale # _____ Time of day _____

What I feel? Where in my body do I feel it?
What I think? What I did?
Write or draw what you notice...

MESSAGE
TO MYSELF

*Write or draw here one
thing I found beautiful today...*

OUTER WEATHER

Day 17

Beaufort Scale # _____ Time of day _____

What can you see? What can you hear?
What can you feel?
Write or draw your observations...

Day _____

Date _____

INNER WEATHER

Beaufort Scale # _____ Time of day _____

What I feel? Where in my body do I feel it?
What I think? What I did?
Write or draw what you notice...

MESSAGE
TO MYSELF

*Write or draw here one
thing I found beautiful today...*

LOOK AT THE
STARS!

Look, look up at

THE SKIES!

—Gerard Manley Hopkins
from the poem "The Starlight Night"

OUTER WEATHER

Beaufort Scale # _____ Time of day _____

What can you see? What can you hear?
What can you feel?
Write or draw your observations...

Day 18

Day _____

Date _____

INNER WEATHER

Beaufort Scale # _____ Time of day _____

What I feel? Where in my body do I feel it?
What I think? What I did?
Write or draw what you notice...

MESSAGE
TO MYSELF

*Write or draw here one
thing I found beautiful today...*

"BUT LOOK

HOW FAR

we've come!"

SAID THE CHILD.

—Russell Hoban

OUTER WEATHER

Beaufort Scale # _____ Time of day _____

What can you see? What can you hear?
What can you feel?
Write or draw your observations...

Day 19

Day _____

Date _____

INNER WEATHER

Beaufort Scale # _____ Time of day _____

What I feel? Where in my body do I feel it?
What I think? What I did?
Write or draw what you notice...

MESSAGE
TO MYSELF

*Write or draw here one
thing I found beautiful today...*

OUTER WEATHER

Day 20

Beaufort Scale # _____ Time of day _____

What can you see? What can you hear?
What can you feel?
Write or draw your observations...

Day _____

Date _____

INNER WEATHER

Beaufort Scale # _____ Time of day _____

What I feel? Where in my body do I feel it?
What I think? What I did?
Write or draw what you notice...

MESSAGE
TO MYSELF

*Write or draw here one
thing I found beautiful today...*

I DON'T KNOW WHERE

I'M GOING

from here, but I

PROMISE

I WON'T BORE YOU.

—David Bowie

OUTER WEATHER

Beaufort Scale # _____ Time of day _____

What can you see? What can you hear?
What can you feel?
Write or draw your observations...

Day 21

Day _____

Date _____

INNER WEATHER

Beaufort Scale # _____ Time of day _____

What I feel? Where in my body do I feel it?
What I think? What I did?
Write or draw what you notice...

MESSAGE
TO MYSELF

*Write or draw here one
thing I found beautiful today...*

Weekly Reflection 3

Write down three small things that went well for you this week.

1.

2.

3.

Write down WHY each went well (this is a crucial step). For example, "I asked for help"; "I arranged to meet a friend for a walk"; "I allowed myself to cry and then had a drink of water," etc.

1.

2.

3.

Write down something you're looking forward to doing in the next week.

MAKE THE

INVISIBLE

visible.

OUTER WEATHER

Day 22

Beaufort Scale # _____ Time of day _____

What can you see? What can you hear?
What can you feel?
Write or draw your observations...

Day _____

Date _____

INNER WEATHER

Beaufort Scale # _____ Time of day _____

What I feel? Where in my body do I feel it?
What I think? What I did?
Write or draw what you notice...

MESSAGE
TO MYSELF

*Write or draw here one
thing I found beautiful today...*

WRITING IS A WAY OF

SAYING

that you and the

WORLD

HAVE A CHANCE.

—Richard Hugo

OUTER WEATHER

Day 23

Beaufort Scale # _____ Time of day _____

What can you see? What can you hear?
What can you feel?
Write or draw your observations...

Day _____

Date _____

INNER WEATHER

Beaufort Scale # _____ Time of day _____

What I feel? Where in my body do I feel it?
What I think? What I did?
Write or draw what you notice...

MESSAGE
TO MYSELF

*Write or draw here one
thing I found beautiful today...*

SOME THINGS TAKE

LIVING

long enough to do.

—Molly Peacock

OUTER WEATHER

Beaufort Scale # _____ Time of day _____

What can you see? What can you hear?
What can you feel?
Write or draw your observations...

Day 24

Day _____

Date _____

INNER WEATHER

Beaufort Scale # _____ Time of day _____

What I feel? Where in my body do I feel it?
What I think? What I did?
Write or draw what you notice...

MESSAGE
TO MYSELF

*Write or draw here one
thing I found beautiful today...*

OUTER WEATHER

Beaufort Scale # _____ Time of day _____

What can you see? What can you hear?
What can you feel?
Write or draw your observations...

Day 25

Day _____

Date _____

INNER WEATHER

Beaufort Scale # _____ Time of day _____

What I feel? Where in my body do I feel it?
What I think? What I did?
Write or draw what you notice...

MESSAGE TO MYSELF

*Write or draw here one
thing I found beautiful today...*

THERE IS A KIND OF

LOVE CALLED

maintenance...

—U. A. Fanthorpe,
from the poem "Atlas"

OUTER WEATHER

Beaufort Scale # _____ Time of day _____

What can you see? What can you hear?
What can you feel?
Write or draw your observations...

Day 26

Day _____

Date _____

INNER WEATHER

Beaufort Scale # _____ Time of day _____

What I feel? Where in my body do I feel it?
What I think? What I did?
Write or draw what you notice...

MESSAGE
TO MYSELF

*Write or draw here one
thing I found beautiful today...*

THE WORK IS

usually

HUMBLE

AND SLOW.

—Piero Ferrucci

OUTER WEATHER

Beaufort Scale # _____ Time of day _____

What can you see? What can you hear?
What can you feel?
Write or draw your observations...

Day _____

Date _____

INNER WEATHER

Beaufort Scale # _____ Time of day _____

What I feel? Where in my body do I feel it?
What I think? What I did?
Write or draw what you notice...

MESSAGE
TO MYSELF

*Write or draw here one
thing I found beautiful today...*

"PAY ATTENTION!"

said the senior

FIREFLIES,

GLOWING BRIGHTER.

—Russell Hoban

OUTER WEATHER

Day 28

Beaufort Scale # _____ Time of day _____

What can you see? What can you hear?
What can you feel?
Write or draw your observations...

Day _____

Date _____

INNER WEATHER

Beaufort Scale # _____ Time of day _____

What I feel? Where in my body do I feel it?
What I think? What I did?
Write or draw what you notice...

MESSAGE
TO MYSELF

*Write or draw here one
thing I found beautiful today...*

Weekly Reflection 4

Write down three small things that went well for you this week.

1.

2.

3.

Write down WHY each went well (this is a crucial step). For example,
"I asked for help"; "I arranged to meet a friend for a walk"; "I allowed
myself to cry and then had a drink of water," etc.

1.

2.

3.

Write down something you're looking forward to doing in the next week.

THE KEY WAS

offered to the

DOOR

MANY TIMES.

—Shem Caulfield

OUTER WEATHER

Beaufort Scale # _____ Time of day _____

What can you see? What can you hear?
What can you feel?
Write or draw your observations...

Day 29

Day _____

Date _____

INNER WEATHER

Beaufort Scale # _____ Time of day _____

What I feel? Where in my body do I feel it?
What I think? What I did?
Write or draw what you notice...

MESSAGE
TO MYSELF

*Write or draw here one
thing I found beautiful today...*

OUTER WEATHER

Day 30

Beaufort Scale # _____ Time of day _____

What can you see? What can you hear?
What can you feel?
Write or draw your observations...

Day _____

Date _____

INNER WEATHER

Beaufort Scale # _____ Time of day _____

What I feel? Where in my body do I feel it?
What I think? What I did?
Write or draw what you notice...

MESSAGE
TO MYSELF

*Write or draw here one
thing I found beautiful today...*

GO AND LOOK

again at the

ROSES.

—Antoine de Saint-Exupéry

OUTER WEATHER

Beaufort Scale # _____ Time of day _____

What can you see? What can you hear?
What can you feel?
Write or draw your observations...

Day 31

Day _____

Date _____

INNER WEATHER

Beaufort Scale # _____ Time of day _____

What I feel? Where in my body do I feel it?
What I think? What I did?
Write or draw what you notice...

MESSAGE
TO MYSELF

*Write or draw here one
thing I found beautiful today...*

IT IS A RELIEF

to follow a

PATH–

SOLID GROUND.

—Dára McAnulty

OUTER WEATHER

Day 32

Beaufort Scale # _____ Time of day _____

What can you see? What can you hear?
What can you feel?
Write or draw your observations...

Day _____

Date _____

INNER WEATHER

Beaufort Scale # _____ Time of day _____

What I feel? Where in my body do I feel it?
What I think? What I did?
Write or draw what you notice...

MESSAGE
TO MYSELF

*Write or draw here one
thing I found beautiful today...*

A RED WING

ROSE IN

the darkness.

—Czeslaw Milosz,
from the poem "Encounter"

OUTER WEATHER

Beaufort Scale # _____ Time of day _____

What can you see? What can you hear?
What can you feel?
Write or draw your observations...

Day 33

Day _____

Date _____

INNER WEATHER

Beaufort Scale # _____ Time of day _____

What I feel? Where in my body do I feel it?
What I think? What I did?
Write or draw what you notice...

MESSAGE
TO MYSELF

*Write or draw here one
thing I found beautiful today...*

FOR THE PRESENT

there is just one

MOON...

—Michael Donaghy,
from the poem "The Present"

OUTER WEATHER

Beaufort Scale # _____ Time of day _____

What can you see? What can you hear?
What can you feel?
Write or draw your observations...

Day 34

Day _____

Date _____

INNER WEATHER

Beaufort Scale # _____ Time of day _____

What I feel? Where in my body do I feel it?
What I think? What I did?
Write or draw what you notice...

MESSAGE
TO MYSELF

*Write or draw here one
thing I found beautiful today...*

FROM TIME TO TIME

OUR LOVE

is like a sail...

—Alice Oswald,
from the poem "Wedding"

OUTER WEATHER

Beaufort Scale # _____ Time of day _____

What can you see? What can you hear?
What can you feel?
Write or draw your observations...

Day 35

Day _____

Date _____

INNER WEATHER

Beaufort Scale # _____ Time of day _____

What I feel? Where in my body do I feel it?
What I think? What I did?
Write or draw what you notice...

MESSAGE
TO MYSELF

*Write or draw here one
thing I found beautiful today...*

Weekly Reflection 5

Write down three small things that went well for you this week.

1.

2.

3.

Write down WHY each went well (this is a crucial step). For example, "I asked for help"; "I arranged to meet a friend for a walk"; "I allowed myself to cry and then had a drink of water," etc.

1.

2.

3.

Write down something you're looking forward to doing in the next week.

THE WIND... RIPPLED AND

FLUTTERED

like light linen, one

COULD FEEL THE FOLDS AND

BRAIDS OF IT...

—Gerard Manley Hopkins

OUTER WEATHER

Beaufort Scale # _____ Time of day _____

What can you see? What can you hear?
What can you feel?
Write or draw your observations...

Day 36

Day _____

Date _____

INNER WEATHER

Beaufort Scale # _____ Time of day _____

What I feel? Where in my body do I feel it?
What I think? What I did?
Write or draw what you notice...

MESSAGE
TO MYSELF

*Write or draw here one
thing I found beautiful today...*

THE INTERESTING THING IS WHAT

YOU CAN DO

that you don't know yet.

—Hilary Mantel

OUTER WEATHER

Beaufort Scale # _____ Time of day _____

What can you see? What can you hear?
What can you feel?
Write or draw your observations...

Day 37

Day _____

Date _____

INNER WEATHER

Beaufort Scale # _____ Time of day _____

What I feel? Where in my body do I feel it?
What I think? What I did?
Write or draw what you notice...

MESSAGE TO MYSELF

*Write or draw here one
thing I found beautiful today...*

OUTER WEATHER

Beaufort Scale # _____ Time of day _____

What can you see? What can you hear?
What can you feel?
Write or draw your observations...

Day 38

Day _____

Date _____

INNER WEATHER

Beaufort Scale # _____ Time of day _____

What I feel? Where in my body do I feel it?
What I think? What I did?
Write or draw what you notice...

MESSAGE
TO MYSELF

*Write or draw here one
thing I found beautiful today...*

EVEN NOW THERE ARE

PLACES

where a thought

MIGHT GROW—...

—Derek Mahon,
from the poem "A Disused Shed in Co. Wexford"

OUTER WEATHER

Day 39

Beaufort Scale # _____ Time of day _____

What can you see? What can you hear?
What can you feel?
Write or draw your observations...

Day _____

Date _____

INNER WEATHER

Beaufort Scale # _____ Time of day _____

What I feel? Where in my body do I feel it?
What I think? What I did?
Write or draw what you notice...

MESSAGE
TO MYSELF

*Write or draw here one
thing I found beautiful today...*

OUTER WEATHER

Day 40

Beaufort Scale # _____ Time of day _____

What can you see? What can you hear?
What can you feel?
Write or draw your observations...

Day _____

Date _____

INNER WEATHER

Beaufort Scale # _____ Time of day _____

What I feel? Where in my body do I feel it?
What I think? What I did?
Write or draw what you notice...

MESSAGE
TO MYSELF

*Write or draw here one
thing I found beautiful today...*

THE EPIC IS BORN OF THE

PARTICULAR,

in the observance of detail.

—Shem Caulfield

OUTER WEATHER

Beaufort Scale # _____ Time of day _____

What can you see? What can you hear?
What can you feel?
Write or draw your observations...

Day 41

Day _____

Date _____

INNER WEATHER

Beaufort Scale # _____ Time of day _____

What I feel? Where in my body do I feel it?
What I think? What I did?
Write or draw what you notice...

MESSAGE
TO MYSELF

*Write or draw here one
thing I found beautiful today...*

AND CATCH THE

HEART

off guard and

BLOW IT OPEN.

—Seamus Heaney,
from the poem "Postscript"

OUTER WEATHER

Day 42

Beaufort Scale # _____ Time of day _____

What can you see? What can you hear?
What can you feel?
Write or draw your observations...

Day _____

Date _____

INNER WEATHER

Beaufort Scale # _____ Time of day _____

What I feel? Where in my body do I feel it?
What I think? What I did?
Write or draw what you notice...

MESSAGE TO MYSELF

*Write or draw here one
thing I found beautiful today...*

Weekly Reflection 6

Write down three small things that went well for you this week.

1.

2.

3.

Write down WHY each went well (this is a crucial step). For example, "I asked for help"; "I arranged to meet a friend for a walk"; "I allowed myself to cry and then had a drink of water," etc.

1.

2.

3.

Write down something you're looking forward to doing in the next week.

THEN IT IS ONLY

KINDNESS

that makes

SENSE ANYMORE...

—Naomi Shihab Nye,
from the poem "Kindness"

OUTER WEATHER

Day 43

Beaufort Scale # _____ Time of day _____

What can you see? What can you hear?
What can you feel?
Write or draw your observations...

Day _____

Date _____

INNER WEATHER

Beaufort Scale # _____ Time of day _____

What I feel? Where in my body do I feel it?
What I think? What I did?
Write or draw what you notice...

MESSAGE
TO MYSELF

*Write or draw here one
thing I found beautiful today...*

YOU HOLD IT LIKE A

LIT BULB,

a pound of light...

—Jacob Polley,
from the poem "A Jar of Honey"

OUTER WEATHER

Beaufort Scale # _____ Time of day _____

What can you see? What can you hear?
What can you feel?
Write or draw your observations...

Day 44

Day _____

Date _____

INNER WEATHER

Beaufort Scale # _____ Time of day _____

What I feel? Where in my body do I feel it?
What I think? What I did?
Write or draw what you notice...

MESSAGE
TO MYSELF

*Write or draw here one
thing I found beautiful today...*

OUTER WEATHER

Day 45

Beaufort Scale # _____ Time of day _____

What can you see? What can you hear?
What can you feel?
Write or draw your observations...

Day _____

Date _____

INNER WEATHER

Beaufort Scale # _____ Time of day _____

What I feel? Where in my body do I feel it?
What I think? What I did?
Write or draw what you notice...

MESSAGE
TO MYSELF

*Write or draw here one
thing I found beautiful today...*

THIS IS

WHAT I'M

noticing...

OUTER WEATHER

Day 46

Beaufort Scale # _____ Time of day _____

What can you see? What can you hear?
What can you feel?
Write or draw your observations...

Day _____

Date _____

INNER WEATHER

Beaufort Scale # _____ Time of day _____

What I feel? Where in my body do I feel it?
What I think? What I did?
Write or draw what you notice...

MESSAGE
TO MYSELF

*Write or draw here one
thing I found beautiful today...*

THE UNKNOWN IS

LESS THAN

I think it is.

OUTER WEATHER

Day 47

Beaufort Scale # _____ Time of day _____

What can you see? What can you hear?
What can you feel?
Write or draw your observations...

Day _____

Date _____

INNER WEATHER

Beaufort Scale # _____ Time of day _____

What I feel? Where in my body do I feel it?
What I think? What I did?
Write or draw what you notice...

MESSAGE
TO MYSELF

*Write or draw here one
thing I found beautiful today...*

...SOMETIMES I GRAB PEN AND

PAPER LIKE AN

utter fool. I have no idea

WHATSOEVER HOW I AM GOING TO

BEGIN AND

what I am going to say.

—St. Teresa of Ávila

OUTER WEATHER

Beaufort Scale # _____ Time of day _____

What can you see? What can you hear?
What can you feel?
Write or draw your observations...

Day _____

Date _____

INNER WEATHER

Beaufort Scale # _____ Time of day _____

What I feel? Where in my body do I feel it?
What I think? What I did?
Write or draw what you notice...

MESSAGE
TO MYSELF

*Write or draw here one
thing I found beautiful today...*

MUCH IS

IN THE

little.

—Horace

OUTER WEATHER

Beaufort Scale # _____ Time of day _____

What can you see? What can you hear?
What can you feel?
Write or draw your observations...

Day 49

Day _____

Date _____

INNER WEATHER

Beaufort Scale # _____ Time of day _____

What I feel? Where in my body do I feel it?
What I think? What I did?
Write or draw what you notice...

MESSAGE
TO MYSELF

*Write or draw here one
thing I found beautiful today...*

Weekly Reflection 7

Write down three small things that went well for you this week.

1.

2.

3.

Write down WHY each went well (this is a crucial step). For example, "I asked for help"; "I arranged to meet a friend for a walk"; "I allowed myself to cry and then had a drink of water," etc.

1.

2.

3.

Write down something you're looking forward to doing in the next week.

WHAT IF...

OUTER WEATHER

Day 50

Beaufort Scale # _____ Time of day _____

What can you see? What can you hear?
What can you feel?
Write or draw your observations...

Day _____

Date _____

INNER WEATHER

Beaufort Scale # _____ Time of day _____

What I feel? Where in my body do I feel it?
What I think? What I did?
Write or draw what you notice...

MESSAGE TO MYSELF

*Write or draw here one
thing I found beautiful today...*

YOUR OWN LIFE WILL

happen to you;

OBSERVE IT.

—Pat Schneider

OUTER WEATHER

Day 51

Beaufort Scale # _____ Time of day _____

What can you see? What can you hear?
What can you feel?
Write or draw your observations...

Day _____

Date _____

INNER WEATHER

Beaufort Scale # _____ Time of day _____

What I feel? Where in my body do I feel it?
What I think? What I did?
Write or draw what you notice...

MESSAGE
TO MYSELF

*Write or draw here one
thing I found beautiful today...*

OUTER WEATHER

Day 52

Beaufort Scale # _____ Time of day _____

What can you see? What can you hear?
What can you feel?
Write or draw your observations...

Day _____

Date _____

INNER WEATHER

Beaufort Scale # _____ Time of day _____

What I feel? Where in my body do I feel it?
What I think? What I did?
Write or draw what you notice...

MESSAGE TO MYSELF

*Write or draw here one
thing I found beautiful today...*

SOME OF WHAT WE

LOVE

we stumble upon...

—Moya Cannon,
from the poem "Introductions"

OUTER WEATHER

Beaufort Scale # _____ Time of day _____

What can you see? What can you hear?
What can you feel?
Write or draw your observations...

Day 53

Day _____

Date _____

INNER WEATHER

Beaufort Scale # _____ Time of day _____

What I feel? Where in my body do I feel it?
What I think? What I did?
Write or draw what you notice...

MESSAGE TO MYSELF

*Write or draw here one
thing I found beautiful today...*

OUTER WEATHER

Beaufort Scale # _____ Time of day _____

What can you see? What can you hear?
What can you feel?
Write or draw your observations...

Day 54

Day _____

Date _____

INNER WEATHER

Beaufort Scale # _____ Time of day _____

What I feel? Where in my body do I feel it?
What I think? What I did?
Write or draw what you notice...

MESSAGE
TO MYSELF

*Write or draw here one
thing I found beautiful today...*

WHAT IS

ALIVE

in winter?

OUTER WEATHER

Beaufort Scale # _____ Time of day _____

What can you see? What can you hear?
What can you feel?
Write or draw your observations...

Day 55

Day _____

Date _____

INNER WEATHER

Beaufort Scale # _____ Time of day _____

What I feel? Where in my body do I feel it?
What I think? What I did?
Write or draw what you notice...

MESSAGE
TO MYSELF

*Write or draw here one
thing I found beautiful today...*

...THE TREES LIKE GNARLED MAGICIANS

produce handkerchiefs

OF LEAVES

OUT OF EMPTY BRANCHES.

—Linda Pastan,
from the poem "November"

OUTER WEATHER

Day 56

Beaufort Scale # _____ Time of day _____

What can you see? What can you hear?
What can you feel?
Write or draw your observations...

Day _____

Date _____

INNER WEATHER

Beaufort Scale # _____ Time of day _____

What I feel? Where in my body do I feel it?
What I think? What I did?
Write or draw what you notice...

MESSAGE TO MYSELF

*Write or draw here one
thing I found beautiful today...*

Weekly Reflection 8

Write down three small things that went well for you this week.

1.

2.

3.

Write down WHY each went well (this is a crucial step). For example, "I asked for help"; "I arranged to meet a friend for a walk"; "I allowed myself to cry and then had a drink of water," etc.

1.

2.

3.

Write down something you're looking forward to doing in the next week.

YES,

and...?

OUTER WEATHER

Day 57

Beaufort Scale # _____ Time of day _____

What can you see? What can you hear?
What can you feel?
Write or draw your observations...

Day _____

Date _____

INNER WEATHER

Beaufort Scale # _____ Time of day _____

What I feel? Where in my body do I feel it?
What I think? What I did?
Write or draw what you notice...

MESSAGE
TO MYSELF

*Write or draw here one
thing I found beautiful today...*

RULE 4: CONSIDER

everything an

EXPERIMENT.

—Corita Kent

OUTER WEATHER

Day 58

Beaufort Scale # _____ Time of day _____

What can you see? What can you hear?
What can you feel?
Write or draw your observations...

Day _____

Date _____

INNER WEATHER

Beaufort Scale # _____ Time of day _____

What I feel? Where in my body do I feel it?
What I think? What I did?
Write or draw what you notice...

MESSAGE TO MYSELF

*Write or draw here one
thing I found beautiful today...*

IN US THERE IS A

RIVER

of feelings...

—Thich Nhat Hanh

OUTER WEATHER

Day 59

Beaufort Scale # _____ Time of day _____

What can you see? What can you hear?
What can you feel?
Write or draw your observations...

Day _____

Date _____

INNER WEATHER

Beaufort Scale # _____ Time of day _____

What I feel? Where in my body do I feel it?
What I think? What I did?
Write or draw what you notice...

MESSAGE
TO MYSELF

*Write or draw here one
thing I found beautiful today...*

OUTER WEATHER

Beaufort Scale # _____ Time of day _____

What can you see? What can you hear?
What can you feel?
Write or draw your observations...

Day 60

Day _____

Date _____

INNER WEATHER

Beaufort Scale # _____ Time of day _____

What I feel? Where in my body do I feel it?
What I think? What I did?
Write or draw what you notice...

MESSAGE
TO MYSELF

*Write or draw here one
thing I found beautiful today...*

NOW

IS THE TIME.

OUTER WEATHER

Day 61

Beaufort Scale # _____ Time of day _____

What can you see? What can you hear?
What can you feel?
Write or draw your observations...

Day _____

Date _____

INNER WEATHER

Beaufort Scale # _____ Time of day _____

What I feel? Where in my body do I feel it?
What I think? What I did?
Write or draw what you notice...

MESSAGE
TO MYSELF

*Write or draw here one
thing I found beautiful today...*

THE TIDE GOES

OUT

and

THE TIDE COMES

IN.

OUTER WEATHER

Beaufort Scale # _____ Time of day _____

What can you see? What can you hear?
What can you feel?
Write or draw your observations...

Day 62

Day _____

Date _____

INNER WEATHER

Beaufort Scale # _____ Time of day _____

What I feel? Where in my body do I feel it?
What I think? What I did?
Write or draw what you notice...

MESSAGE TO MYSELF

*Write or draw here one
thing I found beautiful today...*

IT IS A KIND OF LOVE,

IS IT NOT?

How the cup

HOLDS THE TEA...

—Pat Schneider,
from the poem "The Patience of Ordinary Things"

OUTER WEATHER

Beaufort Scale # _____ Time of day _____

What can you see? What can you hear?
What can you feel?
Write or draw your observations...

Day 63

Day _____

Date _____

INNER WEATHER

Beaufort Scale # _____ Time of day _____

What I feel? Where in my body do I feel it?
What I think? What I did?
Write or draw what you notice...

MESSAGE
TO MYSELF

*Write or draw here one
thing I found beautiful today...*

Weekly Reflection 9

Write down three small things that went well for you this week.

1.

2.

3.

Write down WHY each went well (this is a crucial step). For example, "I asked for help"; "I arranged to meet a friend for a walk"; "I allowed myself to cry and then had a drink of water," etc.

1.

2.

3.

Write down something you're looking forward to doing in the next week.

THE ANSWER TO

"HOW?"

is "Yes!"

—Peter Block

OUTER WEATHER

Day 64

Beaufort Scale # _____ Time of day _____

What can you see? What can you hear?
What can you feel?
Write or draw your observations...

Day _____

Date _____

INNER WEATHER

Beaufort Scale # _____ Time of day _____

What I feel? Where in my body do I feel it?
What I think? What I did?
Write or draw what you notice...

MESSAGE TO MYSELF

*Write or draw here one
thing I found beautiful today...*

KNOW WHEN TO

say "f*ck it"

AND GO FOR A

WALK.

OUTER WEATHER

Day 65

Beaufort Scale # _____ Time of day _____

What can you see? What can you hear?
What can you feel?
Write or draw your observations...

Day _____

Date _____

INNER WEATHER

Beaufort Scale # _____ Time of day _____

What I feel? Where in my body do I feel it?
What I think? What I did?
Write or draw what you notice...

MESSAGE TO MYSELF

*Write or draw here one
thing I found beautiful today...*

WALK ON AND

SEE

a new view.

—Bruce Lee

OUTER WEATHER

Beaufort Scale # _____ Time of day _____

What can you see? What can you hear?
What can you feel?
Write or draw your observations...

Day 66

Day _____

Date _____

INNER WEATHER

Beaufort Scale # _____ Time of day _____

What I feel? Where in my body do I feel it?
What I think? What I did?
Write or draw what you notice...

MESSAGE
TO MYSELF

*Write or draw here one
thing I found beautiful today...*

SUCH WIND IS

WILD

with dream.

—John O'Donohue

OUTER WEATHER

Day 67

Beaufort Scale # _____ Time of day _____

What can you see? What can you hear?
What can you feel?
Write or draw your observations...

Day _____

Date _____

INNER WEATHER

Beaufort Scale # _____ Time of day _____

What I feel? Where in my body do I feel it?
What I think? What I did?
Write or draw what you notice...

MESSAGE
TO MYSELF

*Write or draw here one
thing I found beautiful today...*

OUTER WEATHER

Day 68

Beaufort Scale # _____ Time of day _____

What can you see? What can you hear?
What can you feel?
Write or draw your observations...

Day _____

Date _____

INNER WEATHER

Beaufort Scale # _____ Time of day _____

What I feel? Where in my body do I feel it?
What I think? What I did?
Write or draw what you notice...

MESSAGE
TO MYSELF

*Write or draw here one
thing I found beautiful today...*

PAY ATTENTION, THE

SIGNS

gifted are subtle...

—Grace Wells,
from the poem "Otter"

OUTER WEATHER

Beaufort Scale # _____ Time of day _____

What can you see? What can you hear?
What can you feel?
Write or draw your observations...

Day 69

Day _____

Date _____

INNER WEATHER

Beaufort Scale # _____ Time of day _____

What I feel? Where in my body do I feel it?
What I think? What I did?
Write or draw what you notice...

MESSAGE
TO MYSELF

*Write or draw here one
thing I found beautiful today...*

I HAVE

COME

to discover...

OUTER WEATHER

Beaufort Scale # _____ Time of day _____

What can you see? What can you hear?
What can you feel?
Write or draw your observations...

Day 70

Day _____

Date _____

INNER WEATHER

Beaufort Scale # _____ Time of day _____

What I feel? Where in my body do I feel it?
What I think? What I did?
Write or draw what you notice...

MESSAGE
TO MYSELF

*Write or draw here one
thing I found beautiful today...*

Weekly Reflection 10

Write down three small things that went well for you this week.

1.

2.

3.

Write down WHY each went well (this is a crucial step). For example, "I asked for help"; "I arranged to meet a friend for a walk"; "I allowed myself to cry and then had a drink of water," etc.

1.

2.

3.

Write down something you're looking forward to doing in the next week.

I GO DOWN TO THE EDGE

OF THE SEA.

How everything shines

IN THE MORNING LIGHT!

—Mary Oliver,
from the poem "Breakage"

OUTER WEATHER

Beaufort Scale # _____ Time of day _____

What can you see? What can you hear?
What can you feel?
Write or draw your observations...

Day 71

Day _____

Date _____

INNER WEATHER

Beaufort Scale # _____ Time of day _____

What I feel? Where in my body do I feel it?
What I think? What I did?
Write or draw what you notice...

MESSAGE
TO MYSELF

*Write or draw here one
thing I found beautiful today...*

THE MIND IS A

CHAOS

of delight.

—Charles Darwin

OUTER WEATHER

Day 72

Beaufort Scale # _____ Time of day _____

What can you see? What can you hear?
What can you feel?
Write or draw your observations...

Day _____

Date _____

INNER WEATHER

Beaufort Scale # _____ Time of day _____

What I feel? Where in my body do I feel it?
What I think? What I did?
Write or draw what you notice...

MESSAGE
TO MYSELF

*Write or draw here one
thing I found beautiful today...*

OUTER WEATHER

Beaufort Scale # _____ Time of day _____

What can you see? What can you hear?
What can you feel?
Write or draw your observations...

Day 73

Day _____

Date _____

INNER WEATHER

Beaufort Scale # _____ Time of day _____

What I feel? Where in my body do I feel it?
What I think? What I did?
Write or draw what you notice...

MESSAGE
TO MYSELF

*Write or draw here one
thing I found beautiful today...*

PEOPLE ASSUME THAT TIME IS A

strict progression of

CAUSE TO EFFECT,

BUT ACTUALLY... IT IS MORE LIKE A

big ball of wibbly-wobbly,

TIMEY-WIMEY... STUFF.

—Dr. Who

OUTER WEATHER

Day 74

Beaufort Scale # _____ Time of day _____

What can you see? What can you hear?
What can you feel?
Write or draw your observations...

Day _____

Date _____

INNER WEATHER

Beaufort Scale # _____ Time of day _____

What I feel? Where in my body do I feel it?
What I think? What I did?
Write or draw what you notice...

MESSAGE
TO MYSELF

*Write or draw here one
thing I found beautiful today...*

OUTER WEATHER

Beaufort Scale # _____ Time of day _____

What can you see? What can you hear?
What can you feel?
Write or draw your observations...

Day 75

Day _____

Date _____

INNER WEATHER

Beaufort Scale # _____ Time of day _____

What I feel? Where in my body do I feel it?
What I think? What I did?
Write or draw what you notice...

MESSAGE TO MYSELF

*Write or draw here one
thing I found beautiful today...*

I AM HERE
for the
LIGHT.

—Wim Hof

OUTER WEATHER

Beaufort Scale # _____ Time of day _____

What can you see? What can you hear?
What can you feel?
Write or draw your observations...

Day 76

Day _____

Date _____

INNER WEATHER

Beaufort Scale # _____ Time of day _____

What I feel? Where in my body do I feel it?
What I think? What I did?
Write or draw what you notice...

MESSAGE
TO MYSELF

*Write or draw here one
thing I found beautiful today...*

TRY DESCRIBING WHAT

BEAUTY IS

plainly

AND YOU'LL SEE WHAT I MEAN.

—Dodie Smith

OUTER WEATHER

Day 77

Beaufort Scale # _____ Time of day _____

What can you see? What can you hear?
What can you feel?
Write or draw your observations...

Day _____

Date _____

INNER WEATHER

Beaufort Scale # _____ Time of day _____

What I feel? Where in my body do I feel it?
What I think? What I did?
Write or draw what you notice...

MESSAGE
TO MYSELF

*Write or draw here one
thing I found beautiful today...*

Weekly Reflection 11

Write down three small things that went well for you this week.

1.

2.

3.

Write down WHY each went well (this is a crucial step). For example, "I asked for help"; "I arranged to meet a friend for a walk"; "I allowed myself to cry and then had a drink of water," etc.

1.

2.

3.

Write down something you're looking forward to doing in the next week.

WHERE DOES IT GO WHEN IT

LEAVES US,

the memory of

BEAUTIFUL,

STRANGE THINGS?

—Barbara Kingsolver

OUTER WEATHER

Day 78

Beaufort Scale # _____ Time of day _____

What can you see? What can you hear?
What can you feel?
Write or draw your observations...

Day _____

Date _____

INNER WEATHER

Beaufort Scale # _____ Time of day _____

What I feel? Where in my body do I feel it?
What I think? What I did?
Write or draw what you notice...

MESSAGE
TO MYSELF

*Write or draw here one
thing I found beautiful today...*

...SO YOU CAN LET GO,

NOT JUST TO START THE MORNING,

but to put the last darkness

OF THE ROOM AWAY—

THE NIGHT ITSELF

no more than a start map...

—Jane O. Wayne,
from the poem "When It Lifts"

OUTER WEATHER

Day 79

Beaufort Scale # _____ Time of day _____

What can you see? What can you hear?
What can you feel?
Write or draw your observations...

Day _____

Date _____

INNER WEATHER

Beaufort Scale # _____ Time of day _____

What I feel? Where in my body do I feel it?
What I think? What I did?
Write or draw what you notice...

MESSAGE
TO MYSELF

*Write or draw here one
thing I found beautiful today...*

...AND LIFE SLIPS BY LIKE A

FIELDMOUSE

not shaking the grass.

—Ezra Pound

OUTER WEATHER

Beaufort Scale # _____ Time of day _____

What can you see? What can you hear?
What can you feel?

Write or draw your observations...

Day 80

Day _____

Date _____

INNER WEATHER

Beaufort Scale # _____ Time of day _____

What I feel? Where in my body do I feel it?
What I think? What I did?

Write or draw what you notice...

MESSAGE
TO MYSELF

*Write or draw here one
thing I found beautiful today...*

A BIRD

COMES TO

the window.

OUTER WEATHER

Day 81

Beaufort Scale # _____ Time of day _____

What can you see? What can you hear?
What can you feel?
Write or draw your observations...

Day _____

Date _____

INNER WEATHER

Beaufort Scale # _____ Time of day _____

What I feel? Where in my body do I feel it?
What I think? What I did?
Write or draw what you notice...

MESSAGE
TO MYSELF

*Write or draw here one
thing I found beautiful today...*

OUTER WEATHER

Beaufort Scale # _____ Time of day _____

What can you see? What can you hear?
What can you feel?
Write or draw your observations...

Day 82

Day _____

Date _____

INNER WEATHER

Beaufort Scale # _____ Time of day _____

What I feel? Where in my body do I feel it?
What I think? What I did?
Write or draw what you notice...

MESSAGE
TO MYSELF

*Write or draw here one
thing I found beautiful today...*

"IT HAS HELPED ME," SAID

THE FOX,

"because of the colour

OF THE WHEAT FIELDS."

—Antoine de Saint-Exupéry

OUTER WEATHER

Beaufort Scale # _____ Time of day _____

What can you see? What can you hear?
What can you feel?
Write or draw your observations...

Day _____

Date _____

INNER WEATHER

Beaufort Scale # _____ Time of day _____

What I feel? Where in my body do I feel it?
What I think? What I did?
Write or draw what you notice...

MESSAGE
TO MYSELF

*Write or draw here one
thing I found beautiful today...*

YOU ONLY HAVE
to let the soft
ANIMAL
OF YOUR BODY LOVE WHAT
IT LOVES.

—Mary Oliver,
from the poem "Wild Geese"

OUTER WEATHER

Day 84

Beaufort Scale # _____ Time of day _____

What can you see? What can you hear?
What can you feel?
Write or draw your observations...

Day _____

Date _____

INNER WEATHER

Beaufort Scale # _____ Time of day _____

What I feel? Where in my body do I feel it?
What I think? What I did?
Write or draw what you notice...

MESSAGE
TO MYSELF

*Write or draw here one
thing I found beautiful today...*

Weekly Reflection 12

Write down three small things that went well for you this week.

1.

2.

3.

Write down WHY each went well (this is a crucial step). For example, "I asked for help"; "I arranged to meet a friend for a walk"; "I allowed myself to cry and then had a drink of water," etc.

1.

2.

3.

Write down something you're looking forward to doing in the next week.

NOTHING STANDS

STILL

for us.

OUTER WEATHER

Day 85

Beaufort Scale # _____ Time of day _____

What can you see? What can you hear?
What can you feel?
Write or draw your observations...

Day _____

Date _____

INNER WEATHER

Beaufort Scale # _____ Time of day _____

What I feel? Where in my body do I feel it?
What I think? What I did?
Write or draw what you notice...

MESSAGE
TO MYSELF

*Write or draw here one
thing I found beautiful today...*

MY EYES CAN'T GET

enough of the

TREES

THEY'RE SO HOPEFUL, SO

GREEN.

—Nâzim Hikmet,
from the poem "It's This Way"

OUTER WEATHER

Beaufort Scale # _____ Time of day _____

What can you see? What can you hear?
What can you feel?
Write or draw your observations...

Day 86

Day _____

Date _____

INNER WEATHER

Beaufort Scale # _____ Time of day _____

What I feel? Where in my body do I feel it?
What I think? What I did?
Write or draw what you notice...

MESSAGE TO MYSELF

*Write or draw here one
thing I found beautiful today...*

OUTER WEATHER

Beaufort Scale # _____ Time of day _____

What can you see? What can you hear?
What can you feel?
Write or draw your observations...

Day 87

Day _____

Date _____

INNER WEATHER

Beaufort Scale # _____ Time of day _____

What I feel? Where in my body do I feel it?
What I think? What I did?
Write or draw what you notice...

MESSAGE TO MYSELF

*Write or draw here one
thing I found beautiful today...*

"WELL," SAID FROG, "I DON'T *SUPPOSE* *anyone ever is completely* *SELF-WINDING.* THAT'S WHAT FRIENDS ARE FOR."

—Russell Hoban

OUTER WEATHER

Day 88

Beaufort Scale # _____ Time of day _____

What can you see? What can you hear?
What can you feel?
Write or draw your observations...

Day _____

Date _____

INNER WEATHER

Beaufort Scale # _____ Time of day _____

What I feel? Where in my body do I feel it?
What I think? What I did?
Write or draw what you notice...

MESSAGE
TO MYSELF

*Write or draw here one
thing I found beautiful today...*

OUTER WEATHER

Day 89

Beaufort Scale # _____ Time of day _____

What can you see? What can you hear?
What can you feel?
Write or draw your observations...

Day _____

Date _____

INNER WEATHER

Beaufort Scale # _____ Time of day _____

What I feel? Where in my body do I feel it?
What I think? What I did?
Write or draw what you notice...

MESSAGE
TO MYSELF

*Write or draw here one
thing I found beautiful today...*

THE OPEN SKY

IS AN

empty page...

—Mark Roper,
from the poem "A Far Cry"

OUTER WEATHER

Beaufort Scale # _____ Time of day _____

What can you see? What can you hear?
What can you feel?
Write or draw your observations...

Day 90

Day _____

Date _____

INNER WEATHER

Beaufort Scale # _____ Time of day _____

What I feel? Where in my body do I feel it?
What I think? What I did?
Write or draw what you notice...

MESSAGE
TO MYSELF

*Write or draw here one
thing I found beautiful today...*

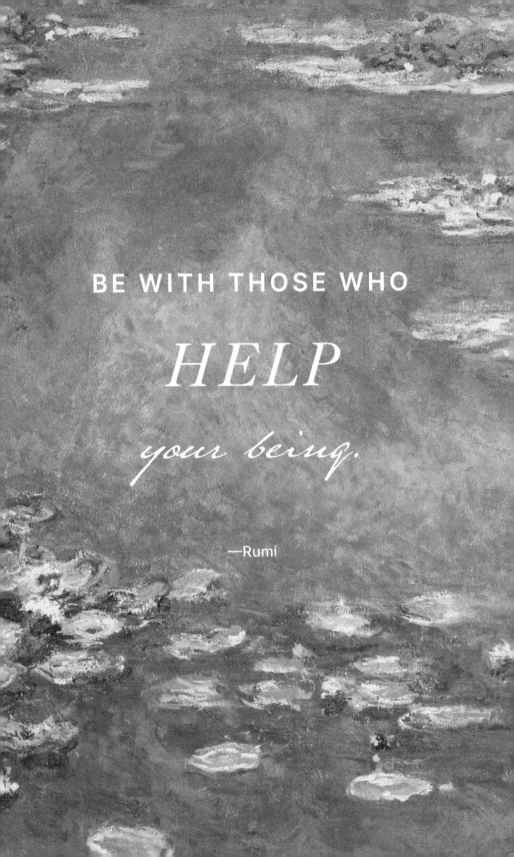

BE WITH THOSE WHO

HELP

your being.

—Rumi

OUTER WEATHER

Day 91

Beaufort Scale # _____ Time of day _____

What can you see? What can you hear?
What can you feel?
Write or draw your observations...

Day _____

Date _____

INNER WEATHER

Beaufort Scale # _____ Time of day _____

What I feel? Where in my body do I feel it?
What I think? What I did?
Write or draw what you notice...

MESSAGE
TO MYSELF

*Write or draw here one
thing I found beautiful today...*

Weekly Reflection 13

Write down three small things that went well for you this week.

1.

2.

3.

Write down WHY each went well (this is a crucial step). For example, "I asked for help"; "I arranged to meet a friend for a walk"; "I allowed myself to cry and then had a drink of water," etc.

1.

2.

3.

Write down something you're looking forward to doing in the next week.

RESOURCE LIST

Here is a list of books that have inspired and delighted me at various times in my life. Some are very recent; others are long-standing companions that I return to over and over. To me these are the kind of books that, having read them, I can gain solace simply from having them on my shelves. They cast good spells. Borrow from mine, or think of compiling your own list, resources that nourish your inner being.

Adler, Tamar. *An Everlasting Meal: Cooking with Economy and Grace*

Armstrong, Karen. *Twelve Steps to a Compassionate Life*

Barry, Lynda. *What It Is*

Berger, John. *Confabulations*

Berger, John. *Ways of Seeing*

Block, Peter. *The Answer to How is Yes*

Britton, Easkey. S*altwater in the Blood: Surfing, Natural Cycles and the Sea's Power to Heal*

Briggs, John. Fractals: *The Patterns of Chaos*

Brunetti, Ivan. *Cartooning: Philosophy and Practice*

De Botton, Alain. *How Proust Can Change Your Life*

De Saint-Exupéry, Antoine. *The Little Prince*

Doty, Mark. *The Art of Description*

Eger, Edith. *The Gift*

Gilbert, Paul. *The Compassionate Mind*

Gregorek, Aniela & Jerzy. *The Happy Body Mindstyle I Got This: The Art of Getting Grit*

Hearn, Lafcadio. *Kwaidan: Ghost Stories and Strange Tales of Old Japan*

Hoff, Benjamin. *The Tao of Pooh*

Jarman, Derek. *Chroma*

Kingsolver, Barbara. *High Tide in Tucson*

Lee, Shannon. *Be Water, My Friend: The True Teachings of Bruce Lee*

Levitt, Peter. *Fingerpainting on the Moon*

McAnulty, Dara. *Diary of a Young Naturalist*

Magan, Manchán. *Thirty-Two Words for Field*

Morris, Ivan (ed & trans). *The Pillow Book of Sei Shōnagon*

Ní Dochartaigh, Kerri. *Thin Places*

Ní Ghríofa, Doireann. *A Ghost in the Throat*

O'Donohue, John. *Walking on the Pastures of Wonder: in conversation with John Quinn*

O'Moráin, Pádraig. *Kindfulness*

Peacock, Molly. *The Paper Garden: Mrs Delany [begins her life's work] at 72*

Scarry, Elaine. *On Beauty and Being Just*

Schneider, Pat. *Writing Alone and With Others*

Shadrick, Tanya. *The Cure for Sleep*

Shepherd, Nan. *The Living Mountain*

Solnit, Rebecca. *Orwell's Roses*

Tarrant, John. *Bring Me the Rhinoceros*

Wax, Ruby. *How to be Human: The Manual*

⭐ ACKNOWLEDGMENTS

Thank you to the many people who joined with me on creative projects over the years. Everything I do has been touched and influenced by so many. The truth about *Weather Report* is that I woke up one morning with the idea of using the Beaufort Wind Scale as a reflective tool. There it may have stayed, simply an idea, if it wasn't for the intervention of Linda Fahy, founder of the Tudor Artisan Hub arts collective, who has a way of making things happen. My nascent idea coincided with a project Linda was beginning to formulate, and it would be the latest in a series of collaborative arts project that we had worked on together over recent years. This time it would be for those in our community of Carrick-on-Suir who had been bereaved of their life partner during Covid-19. This became TOSÚ ARÍS, (it translates from the Irish as, 'starting over'), part of 'Bealtaine', an annual nationwide project in Ireland during the month of May, to celebrate the role of the arts in older age.

Developing *Weather Report* as a prototype for this creative project accelerated its entry into the world much faster than might have happened otherwise. I am indebted to the insight and creativity of illustrator Monty Pyle, who very quickly understood what I wanted in terms of simplicity and delivered such appropriate illustrations. Monty is a student of the Limerick School of Art & Design, Technological University of the Shannon (TUS), Clonmel Campus, one of the creative partners in Tosú Arís. I am honoured that the illustrations here in *Weather Report* now form part of his student portfolio. I am also grateful to Eoin O'Connor, also a student at TUS, who created the wonderful promotional animation for *Weather Report*, which will also form part of his student portfolio.

Special thanks and appreciation to the above mentioned Linda Fahy of The Tudor Artisan Hub for her vision for TOSÚ ARÍS, for her creative input into the prototype of this journal for the Bealtaine 2022 initiative, and for her ongoing support and input in ways too numerous to mention. Linda is an extraordinary creative director, project manager and friend.

My deep appreciation to my fellow members of the creative team on the Tosú Arís project: Eileen Acheson, Eileen Heneghan, Pete Smith,

Sheila Wood; it is always a joy to work with you but especially during the early months of 2022 when we brought this complex and sensitive project from concept to fruition. In addition to your generous and beautiful contribution to Tosú Arís, your responses and generous guidance as you completed your own copy of *Weather Report* during the project, helped me to further refine and polish it. You each shine a bright and generous light in the world, which spills out and makes everything even more beautiful. Thank you all.

Most especially thank you to the six participants of the TOSÚ ARÍS project: Alice, Brian, June, Kevin, Lily, and Madeleine for coming forward to take part in what was a very special healing initiative. You showed me what love and courage could be, what true connection can achieve.

I owe a deep gratitude to the legacy of Pat Schneider, to all in the Amherst Writers and Artists fellowship but especially to Patricia Bender. We first met in Pat and Peter Schneider's home in Amherst some years ago and have been friends and writing buddies ever since, a friendship I value very much. Thank you Patricia for so often being my first reader.

Thank you to my long-standing Book Club friends; Therese O'Neill, Ann Marie Hayes, Geraldine Mernagh and Monica Heynen for being such powerful and inspirational women in my life. Sometimes we even talk about books.

The pandemic period brought many surprises, some of them good. For me these include writing with a group of creatives, a sisterhood of Crows, whose support and companionship deepened week by week as we met each other online through our writing projects. Thank you to Kathy Karn, Beverly Delidow, Cindy Villaneuva, Lisa Orlick, Jackie Alcalde Marr, Joann Malone and Karena de Souza for being the generous wonders that you are. Thank you Tonya Cole, I lucked out in connecting with you and your writing from far (from me) Washington State.

Gail Boenning, writer and chief of the muses, you generously demonstrate what it means to show up every, single day. Thank you for the beauty and thoughtfulness you bring to the world. To Robin Daas, Kathleen Thompson, Susan Lusi, Al Lovelady for continuing to show up with humour and friendship. To Peter Williams for introducing me to the concept of productive accidents; thanks to you I now see such possibilities far more often.

To Nollaig Gallen and Susie Maguire, who showed me what can happen when belief is yoked to action in the world. Because of your energies The Story House Ireland came into being; the doors may be closed, but the ripples are still spreading. I will be always grateful that you both entered my life, with no little wit and style.

Thank you to the wider creative writing community who have formed part of WRITING CHANGES LIVES over the past decade and more; to those who come with their creative energies to my workshops and to the Poetry Plus monthly open mic in the tearoom of Brewery Lane Theatre and to all who form part of the community of this vibrant little theatre. It's about writing, but it's always about more than writing.

To my HAPPY BODY clients, I learn from you every single day that keeping it simple is the very best way.

Many writers whose work has been a source of delight and inspiration to me, who so often showed me the way, have become part of *Weather Report,* either as the quotes sprinkled through the journal or included in the Resource List at the end. Those who know me might wonder how I limited this list, I wonder too. It took superhuman effort and a deadline imposed by Corwin Levi and Michelle Aldredge of Gwarlingo Studio, who I thank for their great eye for composition and harmony that resulted in the book you hold in your hands. A thing of beauty, all I had wished for.

To my four brothers, my Hahessy family of origin, thank you all for being the very best band of brothers a sister could have. I may have been the first-born but I know you've always had my back.

Finally I offer my heartfelt gratitude to my own family. It astonishes me to realise that we now have adult children and that with our grandchildren we are on our 'second clutch', as my dad might have said. *Míle, míle buíochas* to Joe, who walks the path of life with me whatever the weather; *le grá.*

ABOUT THE AUTHOR

Margaret O'Brien is a writer, teacher and creative activist. She has been facilitating writing workshops called Writing Changes Lives for about a decade and a half, based on the radical, empathetic work of the late Pat Schneider. Pat's approach and philosophy is detailed in her book, *Writing Alone and With Others*. Margaret is the founder and curator of the Brewery Lane Writers' Weekend and the open mic, Poetry Plus, both of which have been running in Carrick-on-Suir for over a decade and is Irish editor of the literary journal *Trasna*. She edited the anthology, *Only Connect*, a collection by the Poetry Plus writers written during the pandemic in 2020 and published by Beir Bua Press. Her own writing, both poetry and prose, has appeared in a range of publications. She has previously been a lecturer in Waterford Institute of Technology (now SETU).

In recent years, and especially over the pandemic period, together with the writers from Writing Changes Lives, she has been engaged in innovative cross-disciplinary creative collaborative projects with the Tudor Artisan Hub, an arts collective founded by Linda Fahy and based in Carrick-on-Suir.

Because writers also have bodies, Margaret O'Brien trained as a mentor with The Happy Body, founded and developed by Jerzy and Aniela Gregorek, and takes great joy and satisfaction in mentoring others, helping them to achieve increased physical and mental strength, flexibility and stamina. The Happy Body is a system of physical exercises, based on Olympic weightlifting, which improves strength, flexibility and speed at any age, a practice that she finds to be almost poetic in its completeness. But more than that, it is a way of thinking, a way of living that understands that, "there is overwhelming gracefulness in living *without waste*." Those who practice it find that it's a route to deep health and that it fosters a greater mental focus and also a sense of calmness, qualities that are real antidotes to the pressures and stresses of today's world. The Gregoreks introduced her to the concept of 'triple happiness', which follows from the daily practice of The Happy Body:

"First, you're happy because of the results: you're more youthful and stronger. Second, you're happy because you're the one who achieved your goal; you're proud of staying on course. And third, this happiness radiates out to others, increasing the joy around you." (Gregoreks, *I Got This: The Art of Getting Grit*)

You can find more details of her work at www.margaretaobrien.com

Lightning Source UK Ltd.
Milton Keynes UK
UKHW021655111222
413755UK00011B/80